Mexico

Includes Five SAT Words to Know

IT'S YOUR WORLD
LIVE · WORK · PLAY · LEARN
Where Do You Want to Go?

A Colorful Land of Exotic Culture!

Hey! It's Chichén Itzá! Do you want to go?

FOOD · CULTURE · CUSTOMS · CLOTHING · HISTORY · LANDMARKS

By Carole Marsh

Live • Work • Play • Learn

GALL⊕PADE INTERNATIONAL

Gallopade International is introducing SAT words that kids need to know in our books. The SAT words in this book have a gray box around them. Students can look up the definitions and increase their vocabulary. Happy Learning!

**Gallopade is proud to be a member and supporter of these educational
organizations and associations:**

Association for the Study of African American Life and History
National Alliance of Black School Educators
American Booksellers Association
American Library Association
International Reading Association
National Association for Gifted Children
The National School Supply and Equipment Association
The National Council for the Social Studies
Museum Store Association
Association of Partners for Public Lands
Association of Booksellers for Children

At the time of publication, all websites referenced in this document were valid. However, due to the
changing nature of the Internet, some addresses may change or the content become less relevant.

It's Your World Books

Africa: A Safari Through Its Amazing Nations!

Australia: The Land Down Under for Mates of All Ages!

Canada: The Maple Leaf Melting Pot Country!

China: A Great Wall Runs Thru It!

Egypt: An Ancient Land of Lore; a Modern Land of Oil and More!

France: The Ooh-La-La Country Everyone Loves!

Germany: The Country of Fairytale Castles and Cutting Edge Science!

Greece: A Volcanic Land of Ancient Olympic Origins!

India: Land of Six Senses and Intriguing Mystery!

Italy: The Country of Amazing Fountains and Awesome Arts!

Japan: An Island Country of Endless Intrigue!

Mexico: A Colorful Land of Exotic Culture!

Middle East: Ancient Countries of Current Events Headlines!

Russia: The Great Bear and Its Dramatic History!

South America: A Continent of Countries of Amazing Proportions!

United Kingdom: The Country of Ships, Sealing Wax, Cabbages, and Kings!

Other Carole Marsh Related Titles:

America's Important Neighbors: Canada, Mexico, and Cuba

Spanish for Kids

Table of Contents:

A Letter from the Author..Page 5

Why Should We Care About Mexico? ....Page 6

Top Fast Mexico Facts..Page 7

Where in the World is Mexico? ....Page 8

Building a Temporary Empire! ....Page 9

The Amazing History of Mexico! .... Page 10

Memorable Mexicans! ....Page 11

Guts and Glory Mexican Style! ....Page 12

Maya, That's Beautiful! ....Page 13

Colorful Character! ....Page 14

Teotihuacán..Page 15

Be Sure to Be Late! ....Page 16

¿ Habla español? ....Page 17

Happy Holidays..Page 18

Mexico on the Walls and in the Pyramids ....Page 19

What's For Dinner? .... Page 20

Taking It on the Chin! ....Page 21

Beach Bumming!.. .... Page 22

Mexico Did It First! .... Page 23

Floating Garden Party! .... Page 24

Rio Grande! .... Page 25

Rain and More! .... Page 26

Mexico City—The Heart of Mexico! .... Page 27

Hats Off! .... Page 28

Assorted Architecture!... Page 29

As They Say in Mexico?... Page 30

Further Resources .... Page 31

Answer Key .... Page 32

A Letter from the Author

From the desk of
CAROLE MARSH

Hey kids,

It's your world! It really, really is!
Of course, you already know that, don't you?
You surf the ' net, listen to satellite radio, watch television shows and movies set all around the globe-kids today are much more "worldly" than in the past, and that's a good thing!

Now's a great time to learn something about another country-such as Mexico. Why? Because one day, you might actually visit there (if you have not already!). You might go to school there—many colleges have ties with international schools around the globe. You might even go on to work in a foreign country!

Many companies have positions in other countries. Companies are "going global" as fast as they can. They have branch offices, manufacturing plants, and customer service centers scattered around the globe!

So, ready or not: YOU are a Citizen of the World! And you'll want to be a good one.
How do you do that? You'll find out everything you can about that country, how it's the same, and how it's different from your own country. What language is spoken there? What customs do the people observe? What foods do they enjoy? What do they do for fun? What has happened in this part of the world, and what is happening there now? It's fun ... and the more you learn, the more you will enjoy whatever global opportunity comes your way!

This book is a good place to start your learning journey—so take advantage of the world— IT'S YOUR WORLD, after all ... and guess what? It's a BIG world, after all!

Happy traveling and learning,

Carole Marsh
Always with passport in hand!

Why Should We Care About Mexico?

Mexico is located in the southern part of the North American continent. Mexico is an exotic country filled with a variety of exciting travel destinations. Visitors come to Mexico from around the world! Everyone wants to vacation on the beaches of Cancún, Puerto Vallarta, Acapulco, and Mazatlán, explore the ancient Aztec and Mayan ruins, and so much more!

If you asked where the first university in North America was located, most people would answer the U.S. However, the Royal and Pontifical University of Mexico in Mexico City was the first, founded in 1551. Mexico City is one of the largest cities in the world. It is an important cultural center with more art and historical museums than any other city!

One day, you might visit Mexico to hear the Mexico City Philharmonic Orchestra, explore Mayan ruins in Coba, study at the University of Guadalajara, or work for a Mexican company. It could happen!

Write home about it!
What will your postcard from Mexico say?

Top Fast Mexico Facts!

Important facts to remember about the country of Mexico:

- Mexico's official name is The United Mexican States.
- The currency used in Mexico is called the peso.
- Mexico's form of government is called a federal republic and includes executive, legislative, and judicial branches.
- Almost 93 percent of people in Mexico speak Spanish.
- The country of Mexico is made up of 31 states and one federal district.
- Mexico gained independence from Spain in September of 1810, but wasn't recognized by Spain as being independent until 1821.
- Mexico is slightly less than three times the size of Texas.
- Corn (maize), one of the world's major grain crops, is thought to have originated in Mexico.
- The constitution of the United Mexican States was established in 1824.
- The national anthem of Mexico is "El Himno Nacional Mexicano."

Now, you figure out the rest!

1. This is the Mexican ___ ___ ___ ___.

2. The ___ ___ ___ ___ ___ ___ ___ ___ ___ is Mexico's longest river.

3. Seventy-six ___ ___ ___ ___ ___ ___ ___ of Mexico's people live in urban areas.

4. About 89 percent of the people in Mexico are Roman ___ ___ ___ ___ ___ ___ ___ ___.

5. Mexico celebrates ___ ___ ___ ___ ___ ___ ___ ___ ___ ___ ___ ___ Day on September 16th every year.

6. There are 31 ___ ___ ___ ___ ___ ___ in Mexico.

Where in the World Is Mexico?

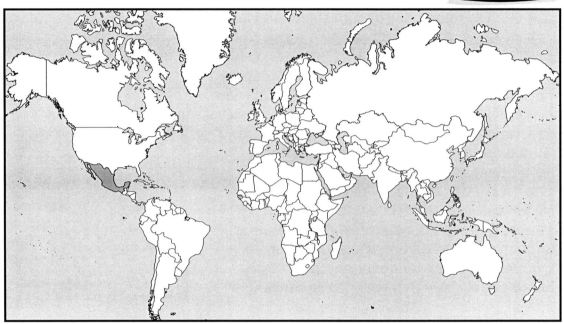

- Mexico borders Belize, Guatemala, and the United States.
- The capital city of Mexico is Mexico City.
- Mexico's coastline borders the Caribbean Sea, the Gulf of Mexico, and the North Pacific Ocean.
- Mexico's total land area is 1,923,040 square kilometers (742,490 square miles).
- Mexico borders four U.S. states—Texas, New Mexico, Arizona, and California.
- The Pico de Orizaba, Mexico's highest mountain peak and North America's highest volcano, is 18,619 feet above sea level.
- The Chihuahuan Desert is larger than the state of California and stretches across six Mexican states, as well as parts of Texas and New Mexico. It is the largest desert in North America.
- The Baja California Peninsula lies between the Pacific Ocean and the Gulf of California.

Do You Know?

1. Most traditional Mexican cuisine is based on the use of this grain:

   a. wheat   b. corn   c. oats   d. rice

2. This U.S. state was a part of Mexico until 1846:

   a. Massachusetts   b. Ohio   c. California   d. Florida

Building a Temporary Empire!

Agustín de Iturbide

Mexico's first empire didn't last long -- just eight months, in fact. That's shorter than a school year! Mexico fought a war with Spain to gain its independence. That war, known as the Mexican War of Independence, went on for 11 long years from 1810 to 1821! It ended when both countries signed a treaty granting Mexico its freedom from Spain.

In May of 1822, the people of Mexico held a demonstration in Mexico City. Soldiers serving under General Agustín de Iturbide, who had fought for the Spanish during the war, led the demonstration. As they marched through the streets, the demonstrators demanded that General Iturbide be appointed to the throne. On May 21, 1822, he became emperor. He gave up the throne a short nine months later on March 4, 1823!

Crosswords!

Use your new knowledge to fill in the crossword puzzle.

Across

2 _____ Agustín de Iturbide originally fought for Spain.
4 The _____ War of Independence lasted from 1810 to 1821.
5 A mass _____ was held in Mexico City in May of 1822.

Down

1 Iturbide abdicated the _____ on March 4, 1823.
3 On May 21, 1822, Iturbide was named _____.
6 Mexico was ruled by ____ until 1821.

The Amazing History of Mexico!

Mexico's history dates all the way back to 8,000 B.C.E. That's ancient! One of the most important civilizations in Mexico's history was that of the Olmec. The Olmec were artists. They created the "colossal heads"—huge human heads carved out of stone!

The Mayan people lived during Mexico's Classical Period from 250 – 900 C.E. One of the Mayans most amazing contributions to the history of Mexico was a fully developed written language. It was the first of its kind in the Americas! Some wonderful examples of Mayan architecture are the many pyramids and religious centers that still exist today.

The most well-known early civilization in Mexico is the Aztec. By the 1400s, the Aztecs had built one of the most advanced societies in all of the Americas! The Aztecs constructed huge temples and sculptures to show their devotion to their gods. The Spaniards destroyed the Aztec Empire when they conquered it in 1521.

Today, Mexico struggles with poverty, immigration, limited health care, and other problems. In spite of that, it remains a vibrant and fascinating country!

Timeline!

Number these events in the order that they took place, first to last.

___ Spaniards conquer the Aztecs

___ Origins of Mexican history

___ Mayan Classical Period

___ Advanced Aztec civilization

___ Olmec settlements are established

Memorable Mexicans!

Mexico

Matching!
Match these famous Mexican people with their accomplishments:

1. _____ I was a Mexican painter and muralist. While living in Europe, I learned the art form called cubism. My wife was also a famous Mexican artist.

2. _____ I was born in Mexico City. I knew by the time I was 11 years old that I wanted to be a chemist! I received my Ph.D. from the University of California at Berkeley, California, and in 1995 became the only Mexican citizen ever to receive a Nobel Prize for science.

3. _____ A Spanish conquistador (conqueror) and explorer, I led an expedition in 1519 from Cuba that eventually led to the fall of the Aztec Empire. After I conquered the Aztecs, I was awarded the title of Marqués del Valle de Oaxaca.

4. _____ I was a Roman Catholic priest. I did not like Spain's dominance of Mexico and led the people to revolt against Spain in 1810. That revolt led to Mexican independence from Spain. I have been called the "Father of Mexico's Independence."

5. _____ I built my first television set at the age of 17. At the age of 23, I received a U.S. Patent for the first color TV system approved by the U.S. Federal Communications Commission! I am also credited with introducing color television to Mexico.

6. _____ I was a Mexican soldier and political leader who became Mexico's first elected president in 1824. I changed my name to show my devotion to the cause of Mexican Independence from Spain.

A. Diego Rivera

B. Mario J. Molina

C. Cortes

D. Father Hidalgo

E. Guillermo Gonzalez Camarena

F. Guadalupe Victoria

Guts and Glory Mexican Style!

A. He was a revolutionary general, a notorious bandit, and a hero to the poor people of Mexico. After years of supporting his fight against the Mexican dictator Huerta, the United States refused to continue supplying weapons to his army. In 1916, he ordered an attack on New Mexico.

B. It is believed to have killed from one-third to one-half of the Aztec civilization in 1520. The Spanish conqerors brought it over from Europe.

C. He was born in 1879 and became a major national hero for his leadership in the Mexican Revolution. He formed and led an army called the Zapatistas and was an ally of the revolutionary, Pancho Villa.

D. This illness usually happens when travelers drink non-distilled water in Mexico. Legend associates the name of the illness with the 9th Aztec emperor of Mexico!

E. This game was first played by the Olmecs in 1000 B.C.E. A heavy rubber ball was used as part of the game and the players wore protective helmets to avoid injury. These noble participants are depicted in carvings from that era.

Mixed Up!
Match the paragraph to the word the paragraph describes.

PANCHO VILLA ____

____ SMALLPOX

EMILIO ZAPATA ____

____
MEXICO'S SACRED BALLGAME

____
MONTEZUMA'S REVENGE

Maya, That's Beautiful!

The peoples of ancient Mexico used simple tools to create some amazing works of art! They used clay, stone, and other materials found near their homes. This artwork helps us understand how the ancient people lived and what they believed.

The ancient Aztecs created art to pay tribute to the gods they worshiped. They used art as a form of communication. Their paintings, drawings, and carvings explain Aztec tribal events and stories. This artwork can still be found today on the walls of ancient Aztec temples!

Another example of ancient Mexican art comes from the Mayan civilization. Like the Aztecs, the Mayan people created beautiful paintings and carvings. The Mayans, however, are best known for their spectacular buildings. They built structures more than 200 feet high. And this was before the invention of the wheel!

Are you an artist?
Get out your crayons. Using the pictures above, draw your own version of ancient Mexican art!

Colorful Character!

Frida Kahlo

The Mexican people love wildly colorful art and their colorful artists! One of Mexico's most famous artists is Frida Kahlo. She painted striking, sometimes shocking images that told the story of her short and troubled life. Originally known as the wife of another famous Mexican artist, Diego Rivera, Frida Kahlo became famous around the world for her own work! Many of her paintings pictured Frida herself wearing traditional Mexican costumes. Frida's creative style included the use of bright colors and symbolism.

Frida was born in Coyoacan, Mexico, in 1907. Frida lived with a lot of pain in her early years. She contracted polio when she was 6, which left her right leg weak. In 1925, a trolley car collided with the bus she was riding. Her painful injuries required many surgeries. She spent many months recovering. While she lay in bed, she painted self portraits using a specially-designed easel and a mirror installed over her bed.

Frida died in 1954. She was only 47. Since her death, her work has been displayed in museums all over the world!

Word Play

Frida Kahlo expressed her feelings in her paintings. Express yourself by using the letters of her name to make as many words with three letters or more as you can.

Frida Kahlo

_____   _____

_____   _____

_____   _____

_____   _____

_____   _____

_____   _____

_____   _____

_____   _____

_____   _____

_____   _____

Teotihuacán

Did you know there are pyramids in Mexico? You'll find them in Teotihuacán! This city was the capital of an unknown people who dominated central Mexico from about 200 B.C.E. to about 700 C.E.

Teotihuacán means "Birthplace of the Gods." Its most impressive structures were the massive Pyramid of the Sun and the smaller Pyramid of the Moon. In fact, the Pyramid of the Sun is the third largest pyramid in the world!

Little is known about the builders of Teotihuacán, including their name, precise religious beliefs, or language.

There is a tunnel directly under the Pyramid of the Sun which leads to caves used for religious ceremonies.

Jaguar heads and paws, stars, and snake rattles are among the images on the sides of the pyramids.

The people of Teotihuacán had hieroglyphics, a calendar, and knowledge about astronomy and herbal medicine.

Pyramids, temples, and single story palaces line the two-mile long stretch called the Avenue of the Dead.

My Favorite Place to Visit!

Create your very own travel pamphlet.
Concentrate on an area that interests you. Perhaps you enjoyed learning about the people. Or maybe it was the monuments that interested you. Fold a piece of paper into three sections. This will give you six areas on which to put information.

Be Sure to Be Late!

Customs and culture vary widely from country to country. Sometimes they vary in different regions of the same country. Here are custom and cultural differences observed by the Mexicans!

- The handshake is a common greeting among men. Women pat each other on the right forearm or shoulder.
- White flowers are considered uplifting.
- It is rude to arrive on time or early for a dinner or party!
- Mexican children don't receive gifts on Christmas Eve or Christmas Day. On the evening of January 5, children put their shoes outside their door, and when they wake up on January 6, the Day of Wise Men, there is a gift in their shoes!
- During a wedding ceremony, the groom gives the bride 13 gold coins as a symbol of his love and trust.
- Most shopping is done in outdoor markets, and arguing about the price of an item is expected!
- The piñata, a hollow figure stuffed with candy, is a tradition at children's parties. Party-goers take turns hitting the piñata with a stick to break it open and release the candy.
- Lunch is the biggest meal of the day, and it is common for people to take a short nap, or a siesta, right afterward.

Create your own!

As we have seen, customs and cultural activities can help define who we are. Think about your family and friends and come up with some new customs for everyone to try.

It is bad luck for a broom to touch the feet of an unmarried woman.

© Carole Marsh/Gallopade International • www.gallopade.com • It's Your World: Mexico

¿Habla español?

The official language in Mexico is Spanish. Spanish is one of the romance languages. Spanish nouns are considered either feminine (la) or masculine (el).

Match it up!
Below are some common Spanish phrases or words. See if you can match them to the English word.

azul

rojo

el gato

el chico

la chica

el papel

el perro

el aeroplano

gracias

hola

cat

red

girl

blue

thank you

paper

hello

dog

airplane

boy

Are you talking to me?

Happy Holidays!

CINCO DE MAYO

Mexico has nine national holidays. Schools, businesses, banks, post offices, and government offices are closed on these days. Some of these days are like ours, such as **New Year's Day, Christmas Day, and Columbus Day.** They also have a **Labor Day** and an **Independence Day** like we do, but they celebrate them on different days.

Most people think **Cinco de Mayo** is Mexico's Independence Day. It is actually a celebration of an 1862 victory over the French army in a small town called Puebla. Puebla has the largest celebration in Mexico by having parades and staging a mock-battle.

Mexico's **Independence Day** is celebrated on September 16th. City squares are decorated in red, white, and green. There are festivities, feasts, and fireworks.

Write it down!
Pretend you are visiting Mexico.
Write a letter to your best friend.
Tell him or her about Independence
Day in Mexico. Describe
how it is different from ours.
Describe how it is the same.

Mexico on the Walls and in the Pyramids

Mexico is a nation immersed in tradition of vibrant art, song, and dance forms. It is the birthplace of the mariachi band, and is universally recognized for its rich tapestry of mural painting. Mexico challenges Egypt with its own pyramids.

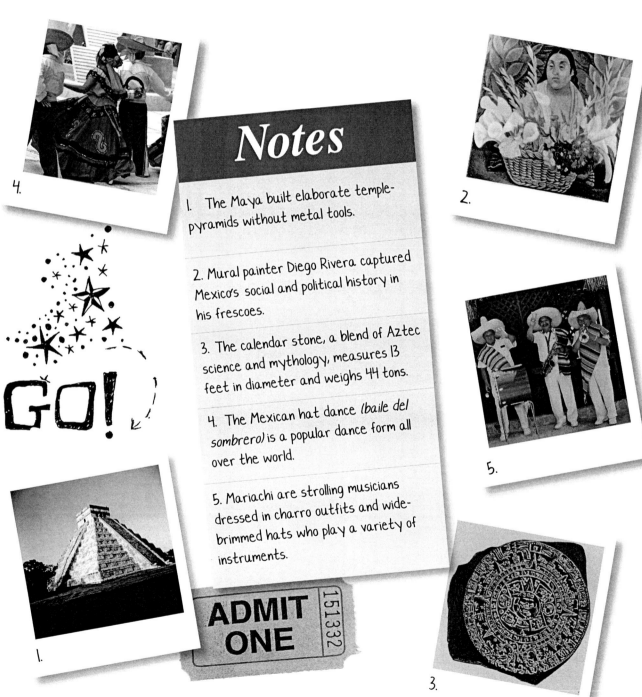

4.

2.

Notes

1. The Maya built elaborate temple-pyramids without metal tools.

2. Mural painter Diego Rivera captured Mexico's social and political history in his frescoes.

3. The calendar stone, a blend of Aztec science and mythology, measures 13 feet in diameter and weighs 44 tons.

4. The Mexican hat dance (baile del sombrero) is a popular dance form all over the world.

5. Mariachi are strolling musicians dressed in charro outfits and wide-brimmed hats who play a variety of instruments.

GO!

5.

ADMIT ONE 151332

1.

3.

What's for Dinner?

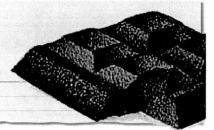

You're probably familiar with Mexican food. Have you ever had a taco or enchilada? Then you've eaten Mexican food! But there are many other kinds of dishes that the Mexican people eat. Take a look below and see just a few.

Tortillas are a type of bread made of flour or corn.

Salsa is a sauce made of tomatoes, onion, chilies, and cilantro.

Mole sauce is made of chilies, spices, and chocolate!

Churros are thick coils of fried dough. They are often dipped in a chocolate sauce—yummy!

RECIPE

Always ask an adult for help when cooking!

Mexican Chocolate Sauce
INGREDIENTS
4 ounces dark chocolate (1/2 cup dark chocolate chips)
1/4 cup heavy cream
1 teaspoon cinnamon
1 tablespoon sugar

MMMMMMMM...this was good!

DIRECTIONS
1. Place chocolate and cream in saucepan over low heat. Stir constantly until mixture is smooth.

2. When it is completely smooth, stir in cinnamon.

3. Pour into serving dish and sprinkle with sugar.

4. Use for an ice cream topper or as a dip for churros!

Taking It on the Chin!

The sport of boxing has a long, interesting, and, in many cases, painful history! The beginning of the sport can be traced all the way back to ancient Rome and Greece. Modern boxing is a combat sport in which two people fight each other with gloved fists. A referee supervises the contest, made up of several three-minute rounds. The referee makes sure the fighters follow the rules. A winner is crowned when either one of the fighters is too injured to continue, or the judges have chosen a winner.

Julio Cesar Chavez Gonzalez

In the mid-20th century, Mexican fighters began to be called some of the best in the world of professional boxing. Julio Cesar Chavez Gonzalez won six world championships in three different weight classes. He also holds the record for 90 wins, one right after the other, without a loss! World champion Salvador Sanchez Narvaez became internationally famous with boxing fans by losing only once in 46 professional matches!

Figure it out!

Figure out the answers to these questions about boxing.

Fast Fact:
The International Boxing Hall of Fame is in Canastota, NY.

1. If a boxing match has 12-three minute rounds, with one minute in between each round, how much time does it take to complete the whole match?

_____

2. Julio Cesar Chavez Gonzalez won six world championships in three different weight classes. How many did he win in each class?

_____

The International Female Boxers Association began in 1997!

Beach Bumming!

   Need a beach vacation? Mexico is home to some of the most beautiful beaches on the planet! Mexico has 9,300 kilometers (5,797 miles) of coastline, which contains a variety of beach destinations.

   Acapulco, located in the state of Guerrero on the Pacific Ocean, is not only a beach resort, but a major Mexican seaport. Archaeological studies have determined that Acapulco has been inhabited since 3,000 B.C.E. It seems the ancient Mexicans liked the beach as well!

   Cabo San Lucas, known as Cabo, which means cape, has some of the most magnificent beaches in all of Mexico. Located at the southern tip of the Baja California peninsula, Cabo San Lucas has become a popular port of call for many cruise ship lines.

   Cancun is a resort visited by almost 4 million people every year. It is located on the Yucatan peninsula. Hurricane Wilma hit this popular Caribbean resort area in 2005. It washed away an eight-mile stretch of Cancun's beach! The area has now recovered, and the beach welcomes visitors once again!

Word Fun!

Place the following beaches in Mexico with their location:

Cozumel, La Paz, Ixtapa, Mazatlan, Puerto Vallarta, Manzanillo, Playa del Carmen

There are more than 20 beach destinations in Mexico!

Pacific	Caribbean	Baja Peninsula
_____	_____	_____
_____	_____	_____
_____	_____	_____
_____	_____	_____
_____	_____	_____

Mexico Did It First!

Word Fun!

This is fun to do with someone else. Ask a friend for words to substitute for the blanks in the story. Their word substitutions will have a humorous effect when the resulting story is then read aloud.

I want to be the first person to _____
(ACTION VERB)

across _____! I've been training for this
(COUNTRY)

since _____. I'm in_____ shape.
(MONTH)   (ADJECTIVE)

My _____ adventure will begin on
(ADJECTIVE)

_____. I won't be hard to miss;
(FAVORITE HOLIDAY)

I'll be the one wearing a _____
(COLOR)

_____ and a pair of matching
(ARTICLE OF CLOTHING)

_____. My faithful friends
(FOOTWEAR)

_____ and
(FAMOUS ATHLETE)

_____ will be there to cheer for me.
(CARTOON CHARACTER)

I'm bringing my _____ along for good luck.
(NOUN)

I'm confident I'll be the first!

Rainbow TV!
Guillermo González Camarena invented the 'color wheel' version of color television. He was also the first to introduce color television to Mexico.

Touchdown!
Rolando Cantu became the first Mexican-born player in the National Football League in 2005.

Mexican Finds Gold in China!
Guillermo Perez won Mexico's first Olympic gold medal at the 2008 Beijing Games, competing in tae kwon do.

That's Some OLD Shade!
Mexico is home to one of the oldest living trees, called "Arbol de Tule." It is believed to be more than 2,000 years old.

Little Lava!
Mexico's Cuexcomate volcano is considered to be the world's smallest volcano, standing only 43 feet tall.

Extra Sour Cream Please!
Ignacio Anaya invented nachos in 1943. He introduced them as "Nachos Especiales."

Floating Garden Party!

Gardens can't float, can they? They appear to be in the southern neighborhood of Xochimilco, Mexico City! There, you'll find more than 50 miles of canals known as the Floating Gardens of Xochimilco! The name Xochimilco means "garden of flowers."

Floating Gardens

This beautiful area is a combination of canals and agriculture. There are two parts to the gardens. The first is a great tourist location where colorful boats called trajineras take visitors through the city canals. Mariachi musicians play traditional music as you ride past historic buildings. Vendors in smaller canoes sell food, drinks, and souvenirs!

The second section of the gardens is an ecology area called Parque Natural Xochimilco. It's home to nearly 270 species of plants and a variety of birds! Here, visitors can learn how the Aztecs created artificial islands out of mud and plants, which eventually became an abundant source of flowers and vegetables for the region. Although the floating gardens of Xochimilco don't really float, the light-weight mud makes them appear as though they are!

Word Fun!
Write five questions about the type of things you might find in the floating gardens.

Example: How many *trajineras* are in Xochimilco?

1. _____?

2. _____?

3. _____?

4. _____?

5. _____?

Rio Grande!

The Rio Grande truly is a *grand* river! Nearly 1,900 miles in length, it is shared by the United States and Mexico—where it is called the *Río Bravo del Norte* (Great River of the North). The Rio Grande was first explored in 1519 by a European expedition surveying the coastline of the Gulf of Mexico.

Even with its grand name and considerable length, the Rio Grande is not a passageway for large ships or even smaller boats. As a matter of fact, because of its low water flow, most parts of the river cannot be navigated at all! The water of the Rio Grande is mainly used to irrigate crops.

Since 1848, the Rio Grande has served as a boundary between Mexico and the United States. Many people from both countries cross it daily. There are five major international border crossing areas along the river between Mexico and the United States.

Most people who cross the Rio Grande into the United States do so with permission. Many others cross illegally to find a better life in the United States. The United States government is working to control illegal immigration along the Rio Grande because every country needs secure borders!

Revealing Answer!

Follow the instructions to reveal the last two words in the complete Mexican name for the Rio Grande.

1. Cross off the first two letters.

2. Cross off the letters M and W.

3. Cross off the seventh and eighth letter.

4. Cross off the twelfth letter.

5. Cross off the fourteenth letter.

6. Cross off the last two letters.

Z A D M W E T Y L N O G R Q T E B Z

Rain and More!

You'll find much more than just rain and trees in Mexico's rain forests! Exotic plants and animals are everywhere! The Los Tuxtlas Biosphere Reserve is home to the northernmost rain forest in the Americas. It is also home to more than 2,700 species of plants and trees, and close to 600 different kinds of birds!

A biosphere can be described as a balanced relationship between humans in the region and the ecosystem that surrounds them. Due to its location, mountain slopes, and wet winds from the Gulf of Mexico, the Los Tuxtlas region has great biodiversity. Nine different types of vegetation have been identified in the beautiful forest. It is also home to:

- 139 species of mammals.
- 160 species of reptiles and amphibians.
- Approximately 350,000 butterflies, which is one of the largest groups of butterflies on the planet!
- 6 major volcanoes, including San Martin, which has not erupted since 1793.

San Martin

Do You Know?
Los Tuxtlas means "place of rabbitts" in the Aztec language?

Cross it off
Starting with the first letter, cross off every other letter to reveal the volcano named in the story.

Z S D A W N T M L A O R R T T I B N

Mexico City—The Heart of Mexico!

Mexico City, the capital of Mexico, is one of the largest cities in the world! It is also one of the oldest! More than 18 million people call Mexico City home. That's more than double the population of New York City! This exciting city was founded by the Aztecs in 1325 and was originally called Tenochtitlan. In 1535, the Spanish conquered the Aztecs and established themselves as rulers. Mexico City was taken over by both America and France in the 1800s and was finally returned to Mexico in 1867.

Mexico City is the seat of Mexico's government, just like Washington D.C. is to the United States! There is plenty to do and see in this amazing city. Cultural and historical attractions include a castle and zoo in Chapultepec Park. The city center has tall, modern skyscrapers, while the floating gardens in Xochimilco display ancient Aztec agriculture.

Mexico City's location high on a central plateau provides good weather year round! From October through May, the weather is especially warm and dry. This capital city has experienced tremendous growth in the last century. Due to the growing population, clean water for everyone is a concern for the future. Despite challenges, Mexico City's future remains bright!

Did you know? Mexico City has more museums than any other city in the world!

Figure it out!

List six museums or historical landmarks below.

1. _____

2. _____

3. _____

4. _____

5. _____

6. _____

Hats Off!

Do you have a favorite hat? Some people like to wear baseball caps, while others prefer stylish knit hats. In Mexico, the traditional hat is the *sombrero!* The name sombrero comes from the Spanish word sombra, or shade. Most sombreros have a high-pointed crown at the top of the hat and an extra-wide brim, which is sometimes turned upward on the edges. *Charros*, or Mexican cowboys, usually wear a sombrero to provide protection from the scorching Mexican sun.

Different people (but usually men) wear different types of sombreros. The sombreros worn by peasants are usually made of straw, while wealthier people have them made from high-quality felt. Stylish! Although they are not common in today's urban areas, sombreros are worn in traditional Mexican celebrations and festivities. Mariachi bands often wear the sombrero during musical performances.

Many visitors from the United States purchase a sombrero as a souvenir of their trip to Mexico!

Dress Up!

Help Christina get dressed for the fiesta! Below are some of the traditional clothing styles you might see in Mexico today. Color the clothing, and draw a line from the piece of clothing to Christina, or cut the clothing out and dress her up.